RAISING A KITTEN

AN ILLUSTRATED KITTEN RAISING GUIDE

By Jonathan Short

Having a kitten brings joy, happiness and an adorable companion who will be loyal for years to come.
In this book we will discuss all you need to successfully raise a kitten and the reponsibilities recquired.

The first step in successfully caring for a kitten is preparing your home! Make sure to safely store any medicines, cleaning supplies and electricity cables.

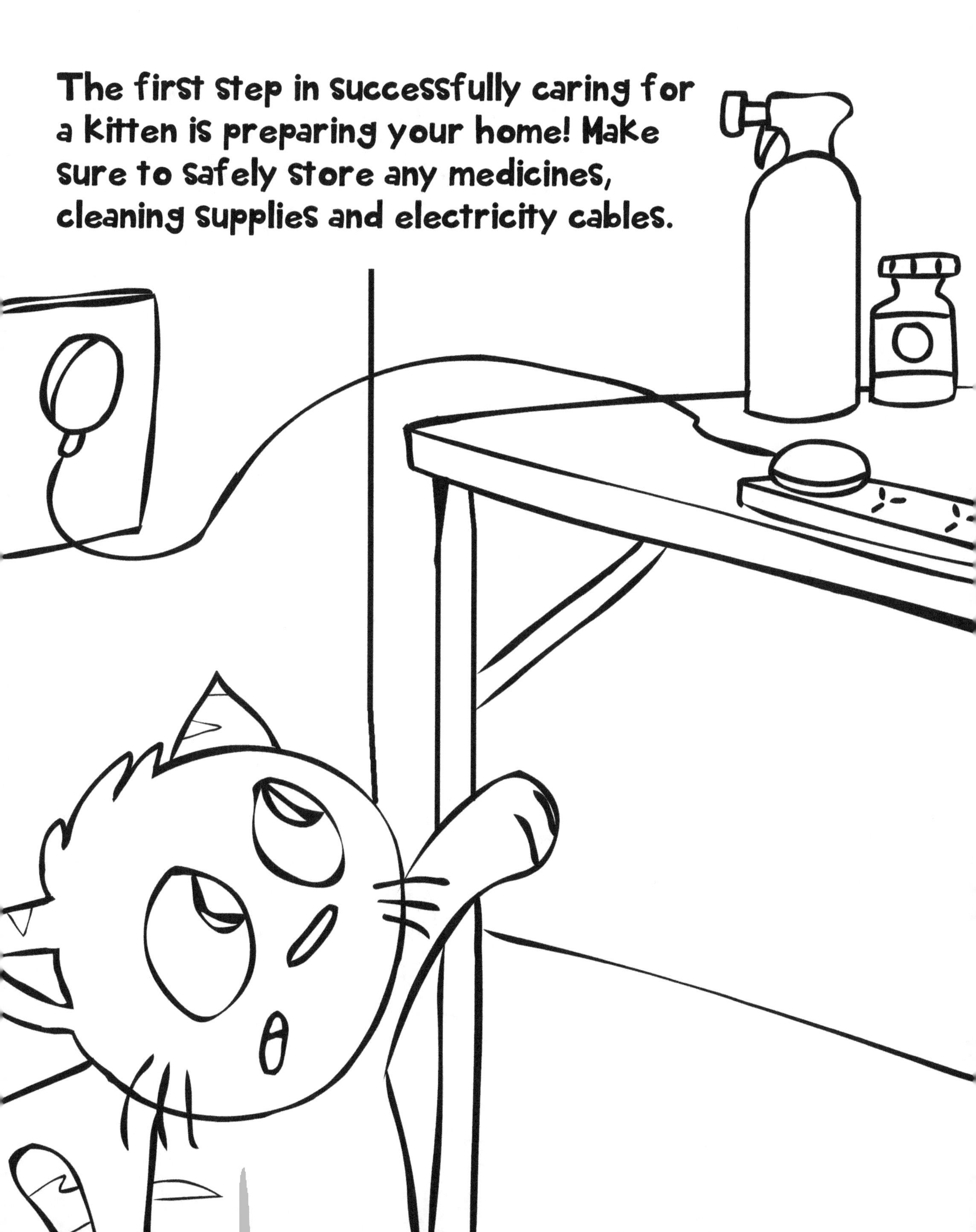

Also make sure they will have no access to
poisonous plants or even that they will not be able
to drink any water from the plant's pot.

When you first get your kitten
they may be a little scared or
nervous so provide plenty of
safe hiding places like cardboard
boxes to give them space.

Start with the same food the kitten was eating before coming to your home. Then slowly introduce new food mixed in if you want them to be on a different food. This will prevent sickness.

Make sure they have plenty of water, stainless steel or ceramic bowls tend to be best as they are easy to clean!

Sometimes pets need time for themselves, so it is good to have safe places for them to go when they feel tired or have had too much attention.

Don't forget a good litter box and plenty of kitty litter for your kitten to take care of their business.

Introduce the kitten to one room
or closed off area that has it's
bed, water and litterbox inside.
Let them get used to this space as
their safe place.
FOOD
WATER

Once your kitten knows where their safe place is with water and tray available, they will become more confident and you can allow them to explore further out into the house.

In the wild a kitten would be learning
to hunt so it is important to give them
plenty of toys to challenge them and
focus that energy!

Scratching posts are also excellent to prevent the kitten from destroying your couch!

Attaching soft toys to pieces of string and attaching them to solid objects also makes great entertainment that will keep a kitten entertained.

Rotating through different toys each day is also excellent as pets can get bored if they have the same toy every day.

Expose your kitten to different sounds, pets can sometimes be terrified of noises like vacuums and hair dryers, so be sure to introduce these and make it a positive experience.

Play with your kitten regularily to burn extra energy, and also to create a stronger bond between the two of you.

Within the first week of getting your kitten, be sure to take them to your local veterinarian.

It is great for them to meet a vet early on and also great to see about your kitten's health.

Be sure to get your Kitten vaccinated and give them worm and flea treatment.

Collars are also great for cats if
they are allowed to go outside.
Just incase your cat gets lost, a
collar with a name and contact
number on it can go a long way to
getting your precious pet back.

If your cat is allowed to go outside, then cat doors are a life saver, rather than hearing your kitten meowing at the door until you open it.

Slowly introduce other pets, when introducing a
kitten to a dog or even another cat. Provide a safe
place for the kitten and keep the dog on a leash.
Be sure they can't physically reach eachother.
Take things slow and repeat, it gets
better over time.

After 8 weeks it is safe to bathe your kitten,
although cats normally clean themselves.
Sometimes your cat may be just too dirty in which
case it is fine to wash them.

After a bath is also an excellent time to brush your cat or in general, some long haired cats may need a brush more than others.

Don't forget to trim your kitten's nails as well as they can become terribly sharp!

Be gentle with your kitten and show them lots of love and they will love you in return!

For Sienna

First published 2018 by Devon Books.

www.facebook.com/devonbooks